T0274903

CLIMATE Change
PROBLEMS and PROGRESS

The Organic Lifestyle

CLIMATE Change

PROBLEMS and PROGRESS

The Organic Lifestyle

James Shoals

Mason Crest

Mason Crest
450 Parkway Drive, Suite D
Broomall, PA 19008
www.masoncrest.com

© 2020 by Mason Crest, an imprint of National Highlights, Inc.

Printed and bound in the United States of America.

Series ISBN: 978-1-4222-4353-4
Hardback ISBN: 978-1-4222-4357-2
EBook ISBN: 978-1-4222-7452-1

First printing
1 3 5 7 9 8 6 4 2

Dreamstime: Phanthit Malisuwan (bkgd); Zilkovec (left); Pablo Hidalgo (right); Jennifer Barrow (bottom).

Library of Congress Cataloging-in-Publication Data is on file with the publisher.

QR Codes disclaimer:

You may gain access to certain third party content ("Third-Party Sites") by scanning and using the QR Codes that appear in this publication (the "QR Codes"). We do not operate or control in any respect any information, products, or services on such Third-Party Sites linked to by us via the QR Codes included in this publication, and we assume no responsibility for any materials you may access using the QR Codes. Your use of the QR Codes may be subject to terms, limitations, or restrictions set forth in the applicable terms of use or otherwise established by the owners of the Third-Party Sites. Our linking to such Third-Party Sites via the QR Codes does not imply an endorsement or sponsorship of such Third-Party Sites, or the information, products, or services offered on or through the Third-Party Sites, nor does it imply an endorsement or sponsorship of this publication by the owners of such Third-Party Sites.

CONTENTS

KEY ICONS TO LOOK FOR

Words to Understand: These words with their easy-to-understand definitions will increase the reader's understanding of the text, while building vocabulary skills.

Sidebars: This boxed material within the main text allows readers to build knowledge, gain insights, explore possibilities, and broaden their perspectives by weaving together additional information to provide realistic and holistic perspectives.

Educational Videos: Readers can view videos by scanning our QR codes, providing them with additional educational content to supplement the text. Examples include news coverage, moments in history, speeches, iconic moments, and much more!

Text-Dependent Questions: These questions send the reader back to the text for more careful attention to the evidence presented here.

Research Projects: Readers are pointed toward areas of further inquiry connected to each chapter. Suggestions are provided for projects that encourage deeper research and analysis.

Series Glossary of Key Terms: This back-of-the-book glossary contains terminology used through-out this series. Words found here increase the reader's ability to read and comprehend higher-level books and articles in this field.

aerobic decomposition the process of degradation in the presence of oxygen

antioxidant a substance that prevents degradation

biodiversity refers to the variety of different organisms present on Earth

cancer a medical condition caused by the uncontrolled growth of cells

compost the organic matter that is fertile in nature

conventional based on the traditional method of doing something

chromatogram a visible record that depicts the separation of elements as per their properties

desiccant a substance that acts as a drying agent by absorbing water

fertilizer the chemical substance used to promote plant growth and provide soil with nutrients

fiber the thin thread used to make cloth

fodder the food for domestic animals

herbicide a chemical used to kill weeds

hormone a chemical substance responsible for growth

irrigation the method of providing water to agricultural fields

leguminous plant a plant that provides nitrogen to the soil

livestock the domestic animals whose products are beneficial for man

mechanical separation separation by hand or simple tools

micronutrients the nutrients required by the body in very small amounts

mulch the organic cover for topsoil to prevent moisture loss

nutrient the chemical substance required by humans to grow and survive

nutrient cycling the process of movement of nutrients through the food chain

pesticide a chemical used to kill insects that attack plants

pollutants the foreign materials which are harmful to the environment

reclaimed wood wood prepared from used wood

recycling the process of using a product again and again in different forms

resistant offering resistance to something

runoff the draining away of water from land surface

tillage preparation of land for crop cultivation

topsoil the topmost layer of soil

weed unwanted plants that grow with other plants and absorb their nutrients

worm casting the fecal matter of earthworms that is rich in nutrients

INTRODUCTION

The increasing use of chemical pesticides, fertilizers, and herbicides harms public health. This was the reason the concept of "Going the Organic Way" was developed. It became highly popular during the 1970s. This concept emphasizes the adoption of a natural way of life. This can be done by using organic products as much as possible. This also has a positive effect on the environment, as organic methods are effective in reducing greenhouse gases such as carbon dioxide in the atmosphere.

Organic farming requires less energy than what is required in conventional farming methods (which lead to the depletion of organic matter in the soil). It increases nutrient cycling, reduces water runoff and soil erosion, and minimizes pollutants. Therefore switching to organic goods is an effective way of reducing global warming.

An Organic Way of Life

Adopting an organic way of life is one of the first steps toward cleaning the Earth of the chemicals it has been exposed to. It also helps the human body get rid of toxic elements, thereby ensuring good health. In addition, it can play a major role in combating climate change and global warming.

Advantages

Organic methods reduce the use of chemicals in our daily lives. The organic ways of producing food and other goods do not involve the use of pesticides, long-chain chemical compounds or **hormones**. They are obtained naturally, and can be easily reused and recycled.

Be Conscious

Gather sufficient knowledge about the labels and certification of organic products. This is important in order to understand the difference between organic produce and conventional produce. An increased awareness about the methods of organic production will motivate more people to go the organic way.

Organic Expenses

Organic products cost more since they are prepared in a unique, pollution-free environment. An organic approach is followed at every step, from producing, harvesting, and processing to the packaging of an organic product.

Climate Facts

- **Recycling** batteries can reduce 165,000 tons of solid waste generated in landfills each year.
- Every year 30 billion tons of top soil is eroded in the United States.

Organic Labels

O rganic labels and certification are the rules created to determine if a product is organic or not. The process regulations are carried out by different organizations in different countries, such as the United States Department of Agriculture (USDA) and the National Organic Program (NOP) in the United States, and Bio Suisse in Switzerland.

Organic Certification

Organic certification is the process of classifying a particular product into various categories as per the percentage of organic elements present in it. The higher the organic content, the more eco-friendly the food product is. All retailers, distributors, and farm owners who are either growing, distributing, or processing organic products must have a certificate for it.

USDA

The USDA implements standards set by the Organic Food Production Act, 1990. The various categories are as follows: 100 percent organic (a totally organic product carrying USDA's Seal), organic (made of 95 percent organic components), made with organic ingredients (at least 70 percent of the components are organic and the rest are from the USDA's list), and natural (may or may not be organic).

Other Labels and Certifications

Different countries have their own ways of certifying organic products. The French certifications are given by ECOCERT, a certification agency that labels organic food products as "AB" and organic skin products as "Cosmebio." In Germany, labels go by the name "Bio-Siegel." In Japan, organic products are labeled "JAS" (Japanese Agricultural Standard).

Climate Facts

- Salt and water are the two items that are not considered for organic labeling.

- In the United States, a fine of $11,000 is imposed if a nonorganic product is labeled as "organic."

Organic Products: Benefits

Products made of chemicals are harmful to human health and the environment. Organic products are produced in an eco-friendly way and are free of toxic substances that harm human health. Thus, "going organic" has become the most natural choice for many people.

Impact on Biodiversity

A recent study has recognized that organic farming produces more biodiversity than conventional farming methods. Insecticides like DDT are harmful to biodiversity as they affect the central nervous system of insects and other animals. Organic products thus help to control pollution.

Toxicity and Pollution Reduction

Only 1 percent of the total **pesticides** and fertilizers used for pest control are used by the plant, while the remaining 99 percent pollute the environment. Organic products overcome this problem as they are produced without using any chemicals.

Impact on Environment

Since organic products are produced without the use of chemicals, they do not contribute to pollution and the release of greenhouse gases into the atmosphere. There is less use of nonrenewable energy in making organic products. Hence, they also help to save energy.

Climate Facts

- Organic food contains essential nutrients, antioxidants, and vitamins, helping the body fight infections better.

- Organic food stays fresh longer even without refrigeration.

Farming

O rganic farming aims at achieving an ecological balance. It involves the use of eco-friendly agricultural practices and avoids the use of chemicals, pesticides, fertilizers, and herbicides. Organic farming helps soil hold moisture and maintain fertility. It is also beneficial to the environment since it controls pollution.

Organic Farming Methods

Crop rotation, do-nothing farming (or natural farming), and biodynamic farming are the various methods used in organic farming. Crop rotation involves growing two crops in rotation, while mulching means adding **mulch** to the top layer of soil in order to prevent moisture loss and to add nutrients. Masanobu Fukuoka, a Japanese farmer, introduced the concept of natural—or do-nothing farming. It involves minimal **tillage** and **irrigation**. Biodynamic farming uses manures and composts as fertilizers. In this type of farming, artificial chemicals are avoided at every stage of crop production.

Maintaining Organic Farms

Organic agriculture is faced with many challenges. The major challenge is soil management, that is, maintaining the fertility of the soil. For this purpose, animal manure, compost, crop waste, and mulch are added to the soil. This is done to add organic matter to the soil. Additionally, **leguminous plants** are grown to supply the soil with nutrients such as nitrogen and potassium. Soil testing is also recommended to monitor soil fertility. Depending upon the results, more raw or composted manure can be added to the soil.

Climate Facts

• A chromatogram helps in differentiating between inorganic and organic food items.

• In 1930, Sir Albert Howard devised organic methods of farming for the first time.

Composting

The process of recycling organic matter, such as animal manure and grass clipping, into **fertilizers** is known as composting. The end product obtained by composting is called **compost**. It is rich in basic **nutrients** that retain moisture in the soil. It is the best way of decomposing the waste in a natural form.

The Composting Process

Composting is done by microorganisms. Microorganisms break the long-chain compounds present in organic matter and release the nutrients. Microorganisms do so either in the presence of oxygen (**aerobic decomposition**) or in its absence (anaerobic decomposition).

Compostable Waste

- Used egg shells
- Garden and pond plants
- Fruit and vegetable scraps
- Leaves and grass clippings
- Animal hair
- Shredded paper
- Soft cardboard

Dairy products, meat, fish, dog excrement, and diseased plants are noncompostable.

Vermicomposting

Vermicomposting involves degrading waste using a variety of worms. Red wrigglers, white worms, and other types of earthworms are most commonly used for vermicomposting. These worms digest the waste and excrete it in the form of **worm castings**. Worm castings are very useful as fertilizers.

How to make a compost pile

Climate Facts

- Earthworms can eat organic matter equal to their body weight.

- Coffee can be used to eliminate odors in compost piles since it acts as a natural deodorant and fertilizer.

Organic Horticulture

The science of growing fruits, flowers, vegetables, and ornamental plants using organic methods is known as organic horticulture. It is usually done with the help of simple hand tools, while avoiding the use of chemicals and fertilizers. The growth of plants depends largely on the soil type, temperature, and rainfall.

Types

Organic horticulture is classified into organic floriculture (growing floral plants which are annual or perennial herbaceous species), organic landscape horticulture (growing floral species that increase the beauty of a region), organic olericulture (cultivation of vegetables), and organic pomology (cultivation, production, and storage of fruits).

Horticultural Rotation

Every organic method of crop production needs a balanced rotation. In the most suitable horticultural rotation, deep-rooted crops should follow shallow rooting crops, and nitrogen-demanding crops should follow nitrogen-fixing crops. Crop rotation is an excellent way to maintain healthy soil.

Useful Species

The choice of species depends on various factors such as soil condition and climate. The most common organically grown vegetables and fruits are apples, melons, carrots, citrus fruits, olives, grapes, cabbage, and cauliflower.

Climate Facts

- A fruit produced from **conventional** farming methods contains more than twenty pesticides even after washing.

- Horticultural rotation helps to control the spread of diseases and weeds in plants.

Organic Gardening

An organic garden consists of organically grown herbs, shrubs, flowering plants, and ornamental plants. Proper testing of soil for its pH, adding compost and organic fertilizers, and controlling pests and **weeds** are essential to ensure the proper growth of plants.

Advantages

An organic garden is the cheapest, easiest to handle, most readily available source of fruits and vegetables. One can be created easily according to available space. Certain vegetables such as carrots are best grown organically as they absorb more pesticides when grown using conventional methods.

Aims

The aim of organic gardening is to preserve the natural balance of the ecosystem as much as possible. Organic gardening emphasizes reduced tillage since mechanical tillage is harmful to the environment. Organic gardeners use organic fertilizers to nourish the soil and plants. As a result, the products of organic gardens are nutritious and safe to use.

Organic Hydroponic Gardening

Organic hydroponic gardening is the latest technique in gardening. It involves growing plants in water instead of soil. In this method, plants are grown in a plastic container filled with water and other nutrients, such as nitrogen (N), phosphorus (P), oxygen (O2), potassium (K), calcium (Ca), and magnesium (Mg). The nutrient medium helps the plants to absorb the nutrients.

Climate Facts

- Organic garden products have 50 percent more nutrients than conventional farm products.

- Cox's apples can be sprayed with thirty-six different pesticides without disturbing the plant cycle.

Organic Food

Organic foods are rich sources of vitamins and minerals and are low in chemical concentrations. Consuming them reduces the risk of several types of diseases. All organic food growers and manufacturers must follow the standards set by their governments and the international organic associations.

More Expensive

Organic foods do not contain chemicals and are grown in small quantities. This is why they can be expensive. Although their production cost is not very high, postproduction turns out to be expensive, as they require chemical-free treatment during harvesting, processing, and transportation.

Types

Organic foods can be grouped into various classes such as organic spices (cumin and coriander), organic herbs (basil and parsley), organic pulses and cereals (rice and pearl millet), organic oil seeds (peanuts, yellow and black mustard), organic/herbal tea (green tea), organic dairy products (milk and cheese), organic vegetables and fruits (cabbage and apples), and organic meat.

Organic vs Nonorganic Food

Regular consumption of organic food prevents **cancer** and heart diseases. These foods are rich in phenolic compounds, **antioxidants**, and minerals, which make them a healthier option. In addition, organic foods are fresh and are more flavorful than nonorganic foods.

Climate Facts

- There has been a drastic increase in the organic food sales from $23 billion in 2002 to $45 billion in 2018.

- Conventional farming uses more than four hundred pesticides to treat different weeds, pests, and fungi.

Meat, Eggs, and Dairy Products

To obtain organic meat and fish, animals are reared without being exposed to chemicals, pesticides, or growth hormones. The animals are kept at a clean place, have limited grazing space, and are vaccinated regularly. Organic meat is rich in vitamin E and essential fatty acids required by the body.

Organic Dairy Products

Organic dairy products are obtained from animals that are raised organically and given organic feed. Several types of organic dairy products like milk, cream, cheese, powdered milk, and organic ice cream are now available. Organic milk is rich in omega-3 fatty acids, is low in antibiotics, and has 50 percent more vitamin E than regular milk. Organic cheese has a perfect blend of omega-3 and omega-6 fatty acids, vitamins A, D, E, and beta-carotene. Similarly, organic lemon verbena and lavender ice cream is prepared using organic sugar, organically grown lavender leaves, lemon verbena, and organic cream.

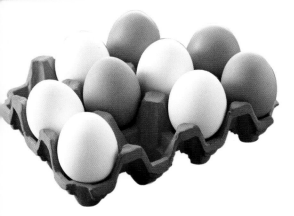

Organic Eggs

Hens that are organically reared and fed with certified organic seeds produce organic eggs. However, hens that are confined to a small place called "free range" may also produce organic eggs, although not always. Organic eggs are rich in vitamins A, D, B9, B12, and B2. In addition to these, they have a high content of choline, which is required by the body for normal cell and nerve functioning.

Mother Earth News: Raising organic chickens

Climate Facts

• Eggs should be eaten with vegetables, as they have no fiber content. Eating them alone can lead to constipation.

• Organic meat tastes better than conventional meat.

GE/GM Food

G E or GM (genetically engineered or modified) food is prepared by changing the genetic composition of plants. These plants are modified in the laboratory to obtain the desired quality. Common modifications include resistance to pests and diseases, increase in nutritional values, and cold tolerance.

GE or Organic Farming?

GE and organic farming are two very different options for the future. Whereas organic farming aims at achieving an ecological balance and promoting **biodiversity**, GE is more issue-specific. GE simplifies complex problems to single issues and looks for a technical solution to the problem. For example, Bt corn releases a toxin that kills a corn pest, the stem borer. However, it can be harmful to certain insects that may benefit the growth of the crop.

Organic farming does not allow any kind of genetic modifications. Organic associations do not approve of GE crops because they believe that such modifications may have severe long-term effects on the consumers, as well as on the soil, and the environment.

Effects on Health

Most GE foods are believed to be safe. However, doctors and scientists around the world are not sure if, in the end, they are harmless. In some places, it has been reported that people have developed allergies after consuming certain GE foods.

Climate Facts

- Organic foods account for only 2.5 percent of the total food sales in the United States.

- Even after several years, organic farms do not leach out minerals from the soil.

Health Benefits

All of us want to have a healthy body. Consuming organic products is one of the easiest ways of attaining good health. Organic fruits, vegetables, and pulses are rich in nutrients, such as iron, phosphorus, vitamins A and C, and in **micronutrients**. Organic meat is the healthiest form of meat.

Nutrition Level

Research shows that organic fruits and vegetables have 27 percent more vitamin content. Organic milk is a rich source of antioxidants, while food items like organic carrots and coriander soup have higher levels of salicylic acid, which reduces swelling and prevents cancer.

A Healthy Choice

Children are more prone to be attacked by toxins, as their tissues are delicate. Thus, the use of organic food is highly recommended for them. Children who consume organic foods from an early age less likely of developing cancer, neurological disorders, and heart diseases.

Is It Really Healthy?

The benefits of organic food for the environment cannot be denied. However, its health benefits have been a subject of much debate among scientists who study organic food. Recent reports in several newspapers suggest that there is little evidence to show that organically produced food is healthier than that produced through conventional farming methods. Also, organic foods are only partially free of chemicals. However, some research has shown that they do contain certain important nutrients in higher quantities.

Climate Facts

- In the United Kingdom, the residues of 31,000 tons of pesticides sprayed on plants each year are found in processed foods.

- According to the EPA, almost 60 percent of herbicides, 90 percent of fungicides, and 30 percent of insecticides can cause cancer.

Organic Pesticides and Fertilizers

Organic food is devoid of pesticides and fertilizers. To raise plants organically, the treatment for pests, weeds, and other microorganisms must also be organic. Several types of homemade preparations such as salt spray, garlic spray, and flour and buttermilk spray are used to rid plants of pests, while organic manure provides the soil with nutrients.

Organic Fertilizers

Organic fertilizers are naturally occurring substances that provide soils and plants with essential nutrients. Many natural fertilizers include manure, seaweed, peat, and worm castings. Organic fertilizers have several advantages. They reduce the risk of over-fertilization by strengthening the physical and biological nutrient storage mechanisms in the soil. These fertilizers consistently release nutrients into the soil, eliminating the need for reapplication. They help improve soil structure and reduce **topsoil** erosion.

Making organic pesticides.

Organic Pesticides

Organic pesticides are the most conventional pesticides. These are compounds that control pests by affecting their normal functioning; for example, tobacco and nicotine spray can be used to get rid of bugs, while plants such as dandelion, Canada thistle, and plantain are used to control weeds. Though derived naturally, there are some organic pesticides that remain controversial, such as rotenone, copper, nicotine sulfate, and pyrethrums.

Climate Facts

- The prolonged use of chemical pesticides damages top soil.

- Tobacco spray, an organically developed fertilizer, should not be used on tomato and pepper since it destroys them.

Clothing

O rganic clothing is made from the material obtained from organic plants and animals. The colors used to dye organic clothes are obtained from natural sources and are devoid of any toxic chemicals. These clothes are easily recyclable and are also environment-friendly. Organic fibers such as organic wool, cotton, and silk are available in many countries.

Organic Wool

Organic wool is obtained from organically raised **livestock**. The animals are given organic food and **fodder**. Navajo-Churro, a rare breed of sheep, is used to produce organic wool. Some of the products made using this wool are baby clothes, blankets, and coats. This wool is also **resistant** to fire.

Organic Cotton

Among all the organic fibers, organic cotton is the most commonly used. It is obtained from organically grown cotton plants. It is widely used to make personal care products, baby products, towels, bed sheets, and blankets.

Organic Bamboo

Bamboo fiber is extracted either by **mechanical separation** or by heating. Bamboo fiber is very soft and has a great ability to absorb moisture. It is used to produce linen fabrics. Clothes made of organic bamboo fabric can be worn in both summers and winters.

Climate Facts

- Bamboo is a grass that grows very quickly, and is ready for harvest in four to five years.

- Every year, twenty thousand deaths occur in developing countries due to the use of pesticides for growing cotton.

Furnishing

Organic furniture is eco-friendly. It is made with non-toxic, organic, and renewable materials. Often mattresses and other pieces of furnishing contain harmful chemicals that can enter our bodies. Organic furniture is made from Earth-friendly materials such as **reclaimed wood**, recycled rubber, and recyclable plastic.

Toxins and Pollutants

Indoor air pollution is caused due to the use of synthetic materials to make furniture, paints, and furniture polishes. Over time, these materials release chemicals, such as radon, formaldehyde, volatile organic compounds, and others. These toxins mostly harm the nervous system of children.

Environmental Impact

The use of organic furniture has a positive impact on the environment. Since it is better in quality and is made of locally grown hardwoods, it need not be imported from other places. Also, since it is made of recyclable materials, it reduces the generation of waste. Organic furniture is often made of recycled items, which thereby curbs deforestation.

Other Furnishing Items

Harmful chemicals used in mattresses and carpets (polyurethane foam, boric acid) accumulate in the human body and act as a **desiccant**. So, natural organic products such as natural wool and natural latex should be used.

Climate Facts

- Between 1980 and 1995, deforestation in almost 772,000 square miles (2 million sq. km) of forest area was observed.

- In 2005, the EPA reported 8.8 million tons of furniture that was discarded in the United States.

Cosmetics

Beauty products are some of the most sought-after organic products. These are developed using natural minerals and organic plant extracts. They do not use synthetic coloring or chemical compounds, and are considered very good for the skin. A wide range of organic cosmetics is now available.

Advantages

Research shows that more than 61 percent of the popular lipstick brands contain lead, which is harmful to the skin. The use of organic cosmetics ensures less exposure to potentially toxic chemical substances. Organic cosmetics are devoid of artificial colors and other harmful substances. They are thick and concentrated and cause fewer skin irritations.

Natural Cosmetics Are Not Organic

"Natural" cosmetics should not be confused with "organic" cosmetics. Natural cosmetics are obtained from plants. These are labeled "natural" if more than 70 percent of their ingredients are derived from natural sources. Although they are made of natural ingredients, they may also be mixed with synthetics. However, organic cosmetics are made only from organically grown herbs, shrubs, and plants. At least 95 percent of the ingredients of a cosmetic product should be organic for it to classify as an organic cosmetic product.

Climate Facts

- One-third of skin care products contain one or more potential carcinogen.

- In the last thirty years, only nine components used in the preparation of beauty care products have been banned.

Organic Movement

The purpose of the organic movement is to spread awareness around the world about organic farming methods and how to adopt them. In the first half of the twentieth century, many organizations and people got involved in the promotion of organic farming practices, since they believed it was sustainable.

History

Many people have made significant contributions to encourage the growth of organic farming. The term "organic farming" was coined by Lord Northbourne, a British agriculturalist, in his book *Look to the Land* (1940). In 1940, Sir Albert Howard, a British botanist, became a supporter of the cause. Influenced by his work and ideas, Lady Evelyn Barbara of England launched an experiment. She cultivated two pieces of land, one organically and the other in a conventional manner. This was the first scientific comparison between both methods of farming. The results of the experiment favored organic farming. This was one of the most important steps in the history of organic farming.

In 1962, Rachel Louise Carson (pictured), an American marine biologist, explained the effects of pesticides on the environment, in her book *Silent Spring*. In her book, she accused the chemical industry of leading a misinformation campaign to make profits. She listed the effects of DDT and other pesticides on the environment. Her work was instrumental in banning DDT in the United States.

Criticism

Critics argue that organic products are expensive, while their distribution is inexpensive. Another argument against organic farming is that it focuses on growing fresh food and not on its taste. However, supporters of organic products have always believed that the health benefits of those products prevail over the disadvantages associated with them.

Organic food: pros and cons

Climate Facts

- It takes between four and five years for a conventional farm to convert to an organic farm.

- The Japanese are the largest per capita consumers of organic products.

Projects

S everal countries have taken up organic projects to study organically produced products. Those involved in these projects study the growth conditions of several crops and their nutrient requirements. The impact of these crops on the environment is also observed.

Fiji Organic Project

The main aim of the Fiji Organic Project is to promote organic sugar, which would be useful for both the environment and the economy. The entire economy of the island is dependent on its sugar export. The aim of the project is to assist Fijian sugarcane farmers to switch to organic production methods and to create a place for themselves in the growing organic market.

Organic Farming in India

The Indian government has started a project with a view to promoting organic farming practices as well as to reduce the burden on chemical fertilizers. Under this project, the government will provide financial and technical support for setting up units to recycle organic waste and for the development of markets for organic products. Another aim of this project is to develop awareness of organically produced products.

Fallen Fruit Project

The Fallen Fruit Project of Los Angeles encourages the sharing of fruits grown in public places. The fruits are grown in an organic manner to benefit the environment, and are good as ornamental plants. The fruits that fall naturally from the trees are collected at night.

Climate Facts

- It takes five hundred years to form one inch (2.5 cm) of topsoil.

- Consuming organic milk lowers the risk of type 2 diabetes.

Baby Products

Young babies are more likely to be affected by diseases due to their delicate organ systems and the tendency to absorb chemicals easily. Thus, a wide range of organic baby products such as soaps, shampoos, baby food, lotions, mattresses, blankets, and toys are being used.

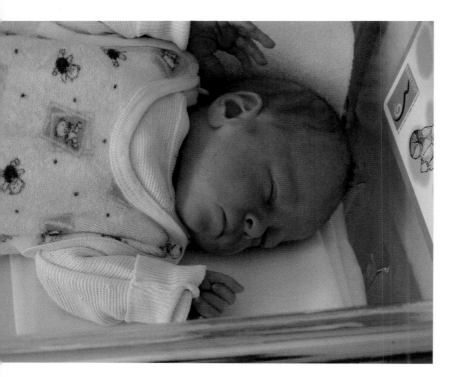

Baby Clothing and Bedding

Organic cotton or organic woolen clothes are suggested for newborn babies. These products are soft and do not cause skin allergies. Also, it is best to use bed sheets and mattresses that are made using organic ingredients since they are soft and do not release any toxins into the air.

Baby Furniture

Organic furniture and other accessories for babies are gaining much attention. Seats, cribs, and other such products are now being widely used by those who support the organic movement and want their babies to be free of toxins. Hammocks and beds made of organic materials are also available in select shops.

Baby Food

Organic baby foods do not contain any chemicals and thereby reduce a baby's exposure to toxic chemicals. It is very important to prevent poisonous chemicals from entering a child's body since it may hamper mental as well as physical growth and the development of the child.

Climate Facts

- Children ages two to four build up six times more pesticides in their bodies than do adults.

- Even diapers made of organic material are now available.

1. What is the USDA and how is it involved in organic foods?

2. What are the benefits of crop rotation?

3. Name three things the text says can be included in a home compost pile.

4. What is hydroponic gardening?

5. What do the food-related initials GE and GM stand for?

6. What do organic pesticides do?

7. In cosmetics, what is the difference between "natural" and "organic"?

8. What chemical did Rachel Carson expose as a huge danger?

RESEARCH PROJECTS

1. Do you have a compost pile at your home? Check out the video on page 17 and the information in this book. Research what you need to start one (ask the homeowner or renter first!) How long did it take for you to get useful soil? Keep a chart of what you put in the pile and how long it took for each product to decompose.

2. Examine the cosmetics and personal grooming products you use. Are they organic? Research substitutes for what you are using among organic products. How much more would it cost you to use organic vs. non-organic? What steps are cosmetics and chemical companies taking to create safer products?

3. Read a short biography of Rachel Carson. How did her book change America and the world? Make a list of 10 other important people in the worldwide environmental movement. Pick one and write a short report to present to your class.

FIND OUT MORE

Books

Barker, David. *Organic Foods (Growing Green).* Minneapolis: Lerner Books, 2016.

Newkirk, Ingrid. *Making Kind Choices: Everyday Ways to Enhance Your Life Through Earth- and Animal-Friendly Living.* New York: St. Martin's Griffin 2013.

Sobesky, Janet. *Natural Style: Using Organic and Eco-Conscious Materials for Earth-Friendly Designs.* East Petersburg, PA: FoxChapel/Creative Homeowner, 2018.

On the Internet

Food Network: Organic Buying Tips
foodnetwork.com/healthyeats/healthy-tips/2009/02/shopping-for-organic-foods

Steps for Natural Living
naturallyfreelife.com/easy-steps-natural-non-toxic-living/

Living Organically: The Organic Center
www.organic-center.org

bioaccumulation the process of the buildup of toxic chemical substances in the body

biodiversity the diversity of plant and animal life in a habitat (or in the world as a whole)

ecosystem refers to a community of organisms, their interaction with each other, and their physical environment

famine a severe shortage of food (as through crop failure), resulting in hunger, starvation, and death

hydrophobic tending to repel and not absorb water

irrigation the method of providing water to agricultural fields

La Niña periodic, significant cooling of the surface waters of the equatorial Pacific Ocean, which causes abnormal weather patterns

migration the movement of persons or animals from one country or locality to another

pollutants the foreign materials which are harmful to the environment

precipitation the falling to earth of any form of water (rain, snow, hail, sleet, or mist)

stressors processes or events that cause stress

susceptible yielding readily to or capable of

symbiotic the interaction between organisms (especially of different species) that live together and happen to benefit from each other

vulnerable someone or something that can be easily harmed or attacked

INDEX

Photo Credits